SONGS

ON THE

PRAIRIE

WIND

Poems of the Land

& its People

Del Cain

Published

2012

Words and Music Press

Saginaw, Texas

contact

del.cain@sbcglobal.net

copyright 2012 by Del Cain

first edition printed 1999

Cover by Alan Justice from a photo by Del Cain edited and
color corrected by Lefty Brandon.

Dedication

This is dedicated to my parents, grandparents, and great-grandparents. They were all pioneers of one sort of another. They all found a place to tie themselves to the land. I am profoundly grateful for what they passed on to me.

Acknowledgments

Thanks to my parents, Elmer and Frances Cain for teaching me by example and story about our family's ties to the land, and especially to Momma for the realization of how the wind sings to us. Thanks to my children, James, Melissa, Daniel, and Christina, who taught me to see how much there is to be learned and to Isabel who taught me what it is to be loved.

I also thank all the poets and writers who have influenced my life and writing over the years including all the writers of DFWWW (www.dfwwritersworkshop.org) and the Austin International Poetry Festival. (www.aipf.org) I must mention my dear friend, fine poet and sharp-eyed editor, Ginnie Siena Bivona and the others of the Tuesday-morning-once-a-month-critique-and-coffee time, Lee Elsessor and Scott Lennox, you are all a constant support, inspiration, and reinforcement to my writing.

To everyone who ever said they liked or were moved by something I wrote, thank you. That's not why I write but it certainly helps keep me going and makes the trip much more enjoyable.

I took the cover picture but it wouldn't have worked without the talent of Lefty Brandon (leftybrandon.com), photographer and friend. Finally, a thank you to Alan Justice for designing a great cover from that picture.

Credits:

These poems first appeared in a chapbook I produced in 1998. A few (very few) changes have been made to correct errors and to improve line breaks. When I decided to update and reissue these I was afraid I wouldn't like them as well as I had so many years ago. I shouldn't have worried. These "Songs" still sing to me and I hope that some of them will also touch you. Some of these have been published in other places and, since that acknowledgment is both morally and legally necessary, the original publication is credited below along with a couple of honors some received.

Sand Plum Jelly, The Watch, and The Sandburrs, first appeared in various issues of Westview: A Journal of Western Oklahoma, published by Southwestern Oklahoma State University Press in Weatherford.

Caught Sleeping by the Windmill received first place in poetry at the 2000, Dallas Writer's Conference.

The Land Was In The Sky and Late in the Season were juried to be read at the Woody Guthrie Festival in Okemah, Oklahoma in 2009.

Table of Contents

Song on the Prairie Wind

So faint at first
I barely hear
the sound insistent
like a cry for help.
I look out the door across
a hundred acres
of cedars and sand plums,
of prairie grass and sage.

Louder now,
I think I hear
my name.
I cross the porch
to cup a handful of sand
thick with memories,
close my eyes
and smell a hundred years
of crops and cows
tended by people
with my mother's name.
Still the murmur comes,
words formed by the breeze
that vibrates through locust branches,

"Write about me,
I gave you your heart."

Winter's Broom

The north wind its broom
winter sweeps its slanted lines
by my window,
blocks sight of the barn
and covers the first board of the yard fence.
Rustler, on the rug by the hearth
jerks and whines and chases
wayward whitefaces
in a dream of spring to come.
My fingers, on their own,
plait the new halter
while I warm
in my own dream
beyond the white drifts
in a pasture of greening grass
and wild flowers
touched by the year's first
soft southern breeze.

Supply Truck Coming In

He was breaking ice so the cows could drink
and stopped to watch his breath
steam into the frozen air.
The air, still as if it were frozen,
carried the rattle of wheels
on the cattle guard two miles off.
Minutes later, straining at the grade,
the supply wagon came up the wash.
Salt, flour, lard, and stuff in cans,
(mostly cans for hands that don't cook much.)
News and tales and a pair of ears
to pour a month's worth of lonesome into.

"Chuck."
"John."
"How ya holdin' up?"
"Fair to middlin', I guess."

As he stacked the cans on rough cedar shelves
the questions he didn't ask came
in a rush and stirred the icy silence.
Maybe by next month the thaw will set in.

Coyote Wind

Coyote wind
slips between my coat and shirt
and nips my ribs
as numb fingers fumble
coat buttons and hood strings.

Coyote wind
howls across the open
and in the draws,
makes winter dry cottonwoods
and cold green cedars
shake and tremble.

He gave us dominion over what we see
but not over the unseen,
the wild and bitter trickster,
Coyote wind.

February Calves

Headed north, old Ginger
must be thinking of the barn
and wants her tail to the wind
instead of head down
hunting a cow too stubborn
to calve in spring
and too smart to stand
exposed to the slicing cold.

When we come in,
she'll be hard to hold
and me too tired
to chase my hat
in frozen mud and snow.
So, I'll rein her in
and with the wind
we'll walk home
to hay and oats,
hot coffee and a fire.

Below Devil's Gap

Below Devil's Gap
in Woodward County
along the North Canadian
my people staked their futures
on twenty cow a section grass
or sand where crops
came the one year
in three it rained
but they raised crops, stock,
children and sand.
Oh, they raised a lot of sand.
They were as prickly
as the sand burrs that
they fought in lawns and gardens.

They followed lonely plows
or rode fence lines
through the snow.
In early days they
kept their rifles close,
together raised the barns
and harvested the wheat
and, like them,
their children's children
don't take much from anyone
but keep a helping hand
below Devil's Gap
in the Woodward County sand.

Grammy 1901-1993

Land cedar dotted,
scarred by blown sand
and sudden rain.
Scarred by tops of oaks
cottonwoods, cedars
peeking out of gullies
where water races only when it rains.

Ninety-two years of rain
and sand and sun
wore gullies
around eyes that saw prairies
from a covered wagon seat
and moon landings on TV
(and knew those fake
to waste her taxes.)
Gullies around a spirit
made hard by hardship
with spots of tenderness
for each grandchild
and grandchild's child
and on into a future
of prairie wind
blowing the red sand.

His Last Mounts

He slowly rocks
in the ragged chair
on an ancient porch
second cup of coffee
cooling in his hand.
Below the silver stars
the prairie's edge fades in
to become the stage to watch
sixty years of ponies ridden,
jugheads and broncs
and cow-smart partners
who found the brush born calves
in draws and gullies
and headed their mamas
to new pastures.

In red spikes
creeping up a cloud
he lives again the noise and dust,
the blood, sweat, smell and squeal
of a calf newly marked
with the brand he rode for.

He has two last mounts,
the mare,
as tired as he,
grain-fed from gratitude,
unridden for years
and the one that slowly rocks him
on the ancient porch.

Trees Have Their Place

Trees have their place
but where I'm from
our fathers planted them early
where they should grow
and generations tended their spread.
They scattered shade on the south
and ordered sentinels
in tight ranks
to stand on the winter sides.
East was clear so morning
could tap on the window
if we should over sleep.

We want to be able
to walk west of
the windbreak line
with the last cup
of a hard day
and lean against the fence
to watch the sun
paint red and rosy streaks
in gilded clouds across the sky.

We don't want shadowed lines,
no dark blots to block the eye
as the last sigh of sunlight
passes the horizon and moves on
to ring morning on some other place.

Promise

A curved dam thrown
across a dry wash,
I don't know when,
before my time,
to catch spring drops
when they fall too fast
to be sucked
into the soft sand.
Now it stands cupping
a green moss wallow
in a red dirt smile
framed by tamarack.

The smile of the sky
at the end of my valley
changes, frowns gray and green
and shouts at me
with a whip crack
and a silver wink
and promises,
like a rich evangelist
or a lightening rod salesman,
something.

Opening the Outlet -- 1893

The border line of eager thousands
stakes in sweaty hands,
weary of the waiting camps,
who survived the thieves and gamblers
who worked the line and
staked their claim to the day and
seized what they could of the
tomorrows of the seekers who made the line.
This land's history already held
the Sooners whose gullies hid them,
Boomers whose voices forced the line,
and those with Outlet claims even
older than the Cherokee whose name
defined the "Strip,"
those so forgotten their loss
was too old to even be a story
told at the campfires
of those who waited
along the simmering line.

Caught In A License Check

Caught in a license check,
digging for my registration,
the cop laughs
and says, That's still
against the law, you know,"
as I toss the old fence cutters
back in the glove box.

Great Granddad, past ninety,
told me how he kept them
in his saddlebags,
not legal in 1880, either,

"A man on horseback can't
always afford to follow fences
when there's work to do.
Let that be the law
you test your honor by
and keep the rest."

So they rattle
against air gauge
and loose change
and strike a note of rightness
that keeps my life
within the fences.

White Faced Babies

Whitefaced babies
ignore mama
like all babies
and run through new green
as I fill feeders with pellets
from my pickup bed.
First day I 've shed my jacket in the open.
The sun's warm handprint
on my back denies
the lies of the north breeze
that nips my ears and whispers
false threats.
Winter won't be back.

The Watch

The horizon line
in the prairie sunset
is erased by gray downstrokes
below the bubbling,
swirling, troubling
of black and green.
The still air
deadens the rumbling
of the dark
and splits itself
into glass stained
with alchemist's art,
lead to gold
fingers searching
for the prairie floor.
The still air
holds promise or threat,
draws by magic
or a call unheard,
prairie people
to yards and porches,
to talk in the hush
and watch the sky.
They breathe what they can
of the pressing air
and wait for the verdict
of the clouds.

Caught Sleeping By The Windmill

Well, he caught me.
Could have,
maybe should have,
thrown my gear in my truck
and me on my way.
Maybe once he ate his lunch
in the spring sun
and lost his way
following a breeze north
as it pushed winter home.
Maybe once he woke up
in a red rush
a the sound of boots
crushing new grass.
Maybe once he had been
tricked to sleep by vanes
that spun and mixed
the sun and blue
and led him, too,
to follow a trail
in a dream.

In Lying Spring

Yellow tipped cedars
softly scrape
branch on branch
in restless air
and turn their heads
back and forth
like the old men
leaning on tractor wheels
scanning the sky
for undelivered promises.

The Grandmother Clock

There it sits,
the Grandmother clock
in its place of honor
on the mantle.
On Sunday I wind it
and all week I hear
it strike away
the hours of my life
as it did for my father
and his grandmother.
She was the canny trader,
Civil War widow,
jewelry maker,
who set practical beauty
to align the hours of 1880
and announce them as they passed.
A child of old cities
nearer the sunrise
she suffered rough prairies
and frontier people
whose lives were so defined
by the making of
one more crop,
one more sale,
they had no spirit left
to iron the sheets and tea-towels
or for the elegance
of carved wood and frosted glass
and the careful tolling
of the hours of life.

The Other Dance

It's not silent in my world.
Streams giggle through sandstone draws
and keep time with cottonwoods and locust trees
that tune their branches softly in the wind.
Feet skitter in the grass
as feathered panic settles
to check themselves in two
or three note syncopation.
A hawk carves curves in unseen air
its cry muted by a breeze.
I want to dance with you
but this is not your music.

The distant roar of trucks
on the interstate echoes
the grumble of diesel boxes
full of people who do not hear
each other or themselves.
Bass thumps and bounces
off marble and shaking glass
and passes by too slowly.
Crowded voices blend, a choir
singing from different scores.

I won't be without you
so I'll dance your dance.

The Place The Light Will Die

The fellow said the blowing sand's
what makes the sunset bright
like a grass fire on the horizon
and for all I know he's right.
What I do know is that folks
coming here from other places
see that red and gold against the blue
and can't control their faces.
They stand and stare at clouds
dyed all those unlikely hues
and wonder why their country's
skies couldn't seem to choose
an even place to let the sun rest
like the line across the sky
that marks the prairie's border,
the place the light will die.

All Those Colors

All those colors
on clouds line up
across the west
reflect the sun shining
on a world I can't,
won't ever, see.

All those colors,
sky and cloud and light
slipping away to visit
day on people I can't see,
who'll never know
I bathed in

all those colors
before they came
their way. I mined
that gold and sipped
that blue and left
no trace of me in

all those colors.
The sky just nailed
my feet to earth
for a moment
before a breeze
urged me back
to my chores.

Sand Fence

The tumbleweed
tumbles across
the baked pasture
to catch in the wire
and snatch grains of sand
from the prairie wind.

One day, soon,
the fence will be
a wave of sand
studded with
cedar post tops.

Sand Plum Jelly

In cabinet rows
like jars of sunrise
that trap the taste
of sand hill summer,
the plain's gift
to the patient
waits for the invitation
of breakfast biscuits.

On winter mornings
its glow and tang
sing of July,
of the sun,
of a land
that gives but
few luxuries
and those are never free.

The Wind Blows

Thank God the wind blows!
Greenhorns whine
because the wind blows,
blows the sand
in my eyes and
the greenhorn's eyes
but I don't whine.
I don't mind the wind.
In the high dry
it lets the shade protect you
from the plains sun
and the posthole digger.
You keep the water jug
in the shade
for an excuse to let the wind
cool the work and
cool your head
but as it blows you cool
it blows you, too
back to the line,
back to your gloves,
back to the diggers,
to build the fence
that, except for catching
a tumbleweed or a few
also won't mind the wind.

Making Hay

The bandana doesn't work,
the hay's in my shirt
and my eyes,
sweat stung,
avoid the line of bales
strung it seems for miles
waiting for the trailer
and me.

My brothers walk the field,
swing the bales
from the ground
for me, the oldest,
to buck in ranks and rows
stair-stepped until the cap row
locks them down
with care.

In the shade of the cedar
in the fence row
the cooler calls.
I don't look.
I can't be first
to call a break, to want a drink.
I grab a bale
to throw

to the top of the stack
to the row in back.
The load's half done.
I've won when John
at the truck door
asks Dad for a rest
and a drink
I wink

at Bob who knows and smiles
and swings another bale
at my feet as water sweet
and cool beckons.
A few more up,
a few more surges
as the urging fence approaches.
Rest comes.

The cool of the water
drunk and splashed,
Joy in the shade
and a crop half made
and cool grass
in the fence row.
A glance at the sun,
"We're burning daylight."
Dad's right.

Great Granddad's 100th Birthday

The horse and mule trader
said, "You're kinda windy."
as I baby-talked on his knee
oblivious to generations that
spread between us and dealt
with other wars than his,
times of cattle drives and
land runs, automobiles and
blowing dust, boom and depression,
airplanes and television.
I was two.
I wish I could remember.
His mind was sharp and clear, they say.
"I wouldn't want to trade horses with him, now"
It made him smile or was he
smiling at Jack Benny on the radio?
This horse and mule man that
hauled supplies for Sherman
to Atlanta and beyond,
this "intruder" in the Chickasaw Nation,
this trader in the motive power
of new territories,
this tenacious spirit that burned
so bright it illumined its frail package
beyond its time.

Prairie Hunter

Feet skitter across the sand
beneath the burrs
the hunter hunts, is hunted.

A gentle bank against the breeze
floats into silent spiral,
drops to the sagebrush floor
then flaring feathers lift
to clear the tumbleweed
and strike.

Talons pull empty
from the sand.
Pinions push the prairie air
to carry aloft
the patient disappointment
of one who did not then
but knows she will...

eat.

The Land Was In The Sky

In New England
We plowed the land
and piled the rocks,
year after year we hauled them
from the furrows and piled them.
It wore my father down
until nothing was left
but to pile the rocks
to cover his grave.

A sign shouted "Free Land!
Free black dirt and red
waits for your plow
to make the grain leap
into sheaves and fill the plowman's
pockets with its gold."
So we went west where they
said there were no rocks
to glean from the furrows
year after year.

I claimed the quarter section
that called my plow
and I challenged my neighbors
to see whose furrow stabbed
straightest into the horizon.
The rain came,
the corn and the wheat grew
and there were no rocks to pile.

Then came the years it didn't rain,
hopes dried up with the land
but the banker carried us,
we bought seed,
we plowed the furrows
that stabbed the horizon
and we were glad
there were no rocks to pile
even in the years it didn't rain.

Just a whisper first, a breeze
that moved a little grit to make
dust devils for children to run through.
Uneasy smiles scanned the sky
in the years it didn't rain.
Harder then, the wind blew and blew,
carried the black dirt and the red.
The sky grew dark
but there were no clouds.
Our wives shoveled dust
from window sills and floors
with grain scoops
that had lost their purpose.
Still we plowed
straight furrows into the horizon
because there was no hope but the land
and the land hoped only for the rain
that did not come, but at least,
there were no rocks to pile.

The wind blew on
until a Sunday when
a black cloud like the
boiling smoke of Armageddon
engulfed the world and
some believed the Temple veil
was rent again and prayed.
Some packed
and headed west once more.
But we stayed
and the banker
in desperate hope
still carried us
though the land was in the sky.

We clung to our dirt
with roots that went deeper than
the wheat or corn
and learned to plow furrows that
helped the land hold on.
We saved the grass
and planted the windbreaks.
We held on,
those that didn't go crazy
held on.

In the first cool, cleansing
drops that fell, we stood,
our faces to the sky
and felt our fears
begin to wash away.

Some cried, some prayed,
some splashed reels
in yards that had not seen mud in years.
I thought of my father,
the way he piled the rocks
and kept plowing.
I think he smiled to see
that when the land
was in the sky
we held on.

Flash Flood

In a dry wash
in the dying light
of a cold steel day
the fallen rider
drags his broken body.
Fear falls like cold steel
clanging on a coffin nail
and the instant river's life
twists fear's knife.

Oklahoma Return

In the red sand
on the red land
shallow rootlets
like locust tree's
hold too lightly
in prairie wind
blowing westward
pushing, moving
the men, not trees,
down the wind west
where no dust dark
brings night at noon
where sun-full sky
drops food on plates
and silver dollars
in the pockets
of those who wait.

Like a catch-rope
their history draws
their children back
to wonder, look,
sometimes to live
in the red sand
on the red land.

Harvest of Hope

No line in the sand
matched the lines on the map
that marked the quarters
the town lots
the school sections
of the Outlet.

"Line up!" they said
for a hundred and sixty
acres of dusty red hope
thick with prairie grass
tumbleweeds and sand plums.

Line up for life
with a dirt floor
and a dirt roof
and one window
looking out on hope
and straight furrows
and grains of threat
catching in the wind
like the tumbleweeds.

Catching on the wing
of the wind of promise,
the wind that will bring
a Black Sunday
to blow hope away.
But still they stay to prove
that they have more grit
than any wind and will not bend
except to plant or pray
expecting the day
work and the sand
bring a harvest to hand.

Sand Burrs

Like sand burrs they came.
Catching rides
any way they could.
Sticking in the sand
with the buffalo grass
they hold the land.
Ancestors of the men
on counter stools
in auction barn cafes
and the worn women who visit
holding the handles of
shopping carts
in the summer cold
of grocery aisles.
Sand burrs still who stick
in the sand
to the land
not hoed out by
hail or heat,
norther or drought,
facing tornado and dust devil
with the same failure to fear.

Who persevere
to hold the land
to root in the sand
and green the spring
and bring blood
from the unwary
who think to pluck
the sand burr
from the sand.

On Grand Dad's Land

Another field of hay put by,
another crop of calves are sold,
another Fall has passed this way,
the morning air is turning cold.

Another year of living made,
another time of blowing sand.
Another child, another colt
to introduce to Grand Dad's land.

Another Winter moving in,
another Spring to contemplate.
Another year of work to plan,
fix the fence and paint the gate.

Another thought matures to dream.
Another child puts out her hand,
another one who bears our name
will build her life on Grand Dad's land.

Late In The Season

Hat pulled down
to shade my eyes
I walk in fading heat.
More than sixty times
I have watched
the signs of seasons pass across
this sand. Now I stand
below the high hill's crest.

Beyond the house
the sun wanders toward
an island of shinnery oak
and startles the underside
of barren clouds
with pink and gold.

I'd best start home. I want
to cross the creek
before it comes full dark.

The Author

My name is Del Cain. I'm a writer of poetry and prose, editor and workshop leader. I live in Saginaw, Texas with my wife, partner, and best friend, Isabel Flores.

I've had a couple of nonfiction books published in the past, Lawmen of the Old West: the Good Guys and Lawmen of the Old West: the Bad Guys and poems and stories in various journals. I'm a life member of DFW Writers Workshop (www.dfwwritersworkshop.org) where, in my opinion, the best support possible for a writer is to be found. I've been involved in various capacities with the Austin International Poetry Festival (www.aipf.org) for years.

I'm a mediocre guitar player, a fair harmonica player, and a beginner on mandolin. In spite of my shortcomings I play all the above with the Common Folk Band. We play country, folk, and a little rock and roll when we play out but we are found every Sunday making the music for the 11:30 am service at Trinity Episcopal Church in Fort Worth.

I like rain, reading, holding hands, horses, guitars, good music, dark beer, dark chocolate, dark nights, and would, almost certainly, like you.

Thanks for reading this and if you have any comments about my work or want to communicate about poetry in general, write me at:

del.cain@sbcglobal.net